ROGUES AND TOADS

Rogues and Toads

A poetry collection

Peter M. Leschak

NORTH STAR PRESS OF ST. CLOUD, INC.

CREDITS:

"Wildland Firefighter" appeared in the Fall 1995 issue of
Lynx Eye.
"Young Logger" appeared in the Fall 1995 issue of
Lynx Eye.
"February Nights" appeared in *North coast Review,* issue
#8, Summer 1995.
"Winter Love" appeared in *The Festival Courier,* 1973.
"Blue Collar" appeared in *Superior Poetry News.*
"Cosmology" appeared in *The Festival Courier,* 1973.
"Advisor to the King" appeared in *Showdown at Big
Sandy;* Doudna, 1989.
"She, My Blood" appeared in *Melting Trees Review,*
Winter 1996.
"Ko Threat" appeared in *Neologisms,* #4, and in *The
American Go Journal,* Vol. 31, Number 3.

First Printing: July 1999

Cover photo: Cecelia S. Dwyer

ISBN: 0-87839-117-7

Printed in the United States of America by Versa Press,
Inc., East Peoria, Illinois.

Published by:
North Star Press of St. Cloud, Inc.
P.O. Box 451
St. Cloud, Minnesota 56302

CONTENTS

ROGUES AND TOADS

WILDLAND FIREFIGHTER

When I imagine fire
I see the sun
Tempered by smoke, and orange
Like a tint of flames on clouds
A pyre for the ennui
Of safety and routine
A serial monogamy
Another dire concubine
To capture me, enthralled
With her hazard and her heat
And the quickening perfume
Of charred spruce spires.
I cherish it too much
The ash and dirt and sweat
Staining faces of my comrades
And admire chronic pain
That proves I'm still alive
Although they call it ugly
There is nothing ever higher
Than the rushing way a conifer explodes.

When I imagine fire
I see the moon
Filtered by smoke, and orange
Like a baleful eye
Of apocalypse.
I desire the worst way up
And no way down
Unless the line is flagged
By Prometheus himself
Or the ghost of E. Pulaski
I require only duty and aspire to only dawn.

When I imagine fire
I see the stars
Magnified in blackness, and bright
Like the glinting lamps of hot shots gone to hell.

SHE, MY BLOOD

The poetry is killing me
Like tobacco, or other congenial addictions
Spilling from pages and appearing
At odd moments, catching memory
Like a glint of sunlight in a window prism
Snares the eye, and thrilling me
With terror
Like a razor pressed to my throat
By a forsaken lover
Willing to paint her face with my blood,
Though such a woman never lived
How chilling and fine
That she and poetry are one
And I am found in words,
Fulfilling yearbook promises
For chump change and wonder.

FEBRUARY NIGHTS

No cynic breath
Rises from my parted lips
Dissipating to starfields
From snowfields,
And no skeptic arms
Stretch to encompass light years
Reaching past dead ends
From bookends,
For I'm a zealot on winter nights
On fire for all that's celestial
Yearning for love songs
Tangling a love knot.

"OH MOTHER! I WAS BORN TO DIE YOUNG!"*

For John Curtis Niemi, 1951-1975

I

I dreamed of falling, was it limbs
That broke without my grasp
The vapor sky was paper thin
I knew it was a trap.
My fingers clutched at molecules
They slid and shot and leapt
The air that scorched my rasping lungs
Ripped at bloodstream depth.
"Wake up you dreamer!" shrieked my friend
The earth with angry rocks
Came twisting toward my spinning eyes
My voice in steel locks
I couldn't shout or even gasp
My terror couldn't cry
I hit the floor and jerked awake,
Achilles didn't die.

II

I blasted John with a plastic gun
He yelled and fell in the grass
But no coffin was laid by the altar
And no one wailed in Mass.
He rose from the dead, aimed his toy
And with a childish laugh in the sun
He cut me two by the fence in the yard
And I never let loose of my gun.

III

An hour before the autumn rain
We viewed John's pallid flesh
The grass was brown and wilted
The spaded dirt was fresh.
No plastic gun had cut him short
But plastic men were there

To curse the bullet in his heart
To leave us chilled and bare.
"How young!" they cried, and
"Damn, what a waste!"
But I smiled at soulward depth,
We plastic men were still ensnared
But, John, by god, had left.

*Achilles, in *The Illiad*

PIRATES

Emaciated shipwrights slaving in the sun
Captain on the quarterdeck in lawless expectation
Steeples in the distance, servants to the shore
Ebbing with the lowest tide away from all the nation.

Artillery into the holds, straining at the ropes
Easy, easy at the winch, see the muzzles gleam
Unleashed from molten riffles, cast out hard and cold
To ornament amidships' ports and fire pirate dreams.

A greedy gaudy regiment, a crew of dungeon rats
For hostile executions of merchantmen and orders
Autocrats of lead and steel, of sandy bloody decks
Princes of the yardarm, crude ferocious boarders.

Superior to the fishermen and strangers to the net
A code of sullied honor familiar with the noose
Prosperous in poverty, exuberant in shame
Halberds for the heads of men, no spirits of the muse.

A navigator at the helm with passion for the stars
Preoccupied with latitude, Polaris and the sun
Who spys no evil in the sky and hears no cutlass ring
Who wields sextant like a sword and compass like a gun.

Cast off and bid farewell to no one on the beach
Benevolence is lost on crows and kisses on corsairs
Who love the sea and plunder, fear the shot and powder
Forsaking all before the mast, a giddy windswept lair.

OUR FLEETING AFFECTION

When I command the greenhorns jump
To it, the grunts fresh enough
To be my own brats
Though I don't demand obedience
But merely attention to details
That keep us all standing
And breathing and provide prospects
Beyond the next shift.

When I command I raise my hand
To only their collars
Grasping shoulders to tie-in,
Scanning their faces for fear
And comprehension
Making sure our eyes share
The same brand of fire
And my words are bullets.

When I command I don't care
About chains or systems
In that instant of touch twisting
A strand of love
For who we are then,
Not in life outside the crew
Where very few understand
How grand is our fleeting affection.

AND SHINING DOVES
(Jude, v. 12,13)

The demons danced in Babylon
In moonlit ruins
In howling strife
The jackals fought for dusty bones
The desert clawed for life.

     A reptile dream of squirming serpents
     Dragons lizards worms and snakes
     Between the bars of an infant's crib
     In heaps of twisting slithering skin
     A shrieking child with pinky fingers
     Grasping bars in a maternal trap
     Garish darkness hears his cries
     But that's what let the reptiles in.

The demons laughed in Sodom's ash
Of smoking hell
Of blackened earth
Licking the salty wife of Lot
They lay choking in their mirth.

     Green stick years rush crashing down
     To halt in caskets neatly laid
     Till curtain time with sacred flags
     Lullabies with bugles and rifles
     Peace on earth in well-kept graves
     Rest in peace but dead in vain.

The demons smiled with Nimrod
At hunted blood
At butchered blame
The mothers wailed to Molech
The demons sucked the flames.

With lamps aloft beneath the stars
Virgin fire, sparkling eyes
Sisters ford the valley streams
And washing feet the Son of Man
Offers waving wheat not grown in fleeting dreams
But harvest life from waning death
And shining doves.
Shepherd-led by spirit words
Not vengeful mercy, human means
Sisters walk another mile
A different mile but all one breath.

The demons cried from drying clouds
Of withered trees
Of foaming guilt
With nothing seen and nothing heard
Lost in wastes that blow and wilt.

SANDRA'S GIFT

Though in a crowded hall
As she danced in our direction
I knew her eyes were aiming right for me
She bubbled with excitement
As she told me with affection
Of some little thing that I would have to see.

And in a crowded world
Where time is only teeming
And faces fade before the night is dawn
I cup her sterling thought
In trembling grateful hands
Before that precious little thing is gone.

UPSTREAM THE ASPHALT DRAINAGE

Riding monotonous wheels
And yes, through stew broth fog
Fourth gear's driving on
Deeper into veils of mist
Which close behind me
But do not open before
I smash them with my brights
Then switch again to lows
Keeping dashes as my partners
The radio as my friend
Morning as my goal.

Aiming for Chicago
Feeling lost on the right road
Found the wrong way
And eaten alive by smog
In the paved throat of a night creature
Heading down and not north
Deep and not south
Straight by spinning
To the pit of digestion
Which will break me down
If I linger too long
In its jostling intestines
Absorbing the juices of its tunnel skies
And being gradually lost among glittering tombs.

Accept me, fog,
And steer me gone yet guided
Upstream the asphalt drainage
Until the dawn-distorted sun will sigh
"Breathe, the danger is past."

A FIREFIGHTER'S CREMATION

When I was young and dreamed of death
On bloodless fields of glory
My face and limbs were key
And gleamed with romantic mortality
That girlish nurses bathed with steamy tears.

But now when I confront infernos
And scheme to cheat flames of middle-aged flesh
I realize the theme no longer requires my corpse
Instead, should death prevail inside some hellish
       hallway
I will not hear of "remains"
And want no scream to point "There he is !"
But find merely a charred end of hose
Perhaps a blackened beam atop an empty helmet,
Tears I no longer need.

SINGERS

Gliders of the snowdrifts
A sphere above the mice
Tracing wispy crystals
To glaze the winter ice
And show the stealthy fox
That my friends and I were by
She'll catch a whiff of scent
But mistake it for the sky.

Singers in the treetops
A sphere above the frost
Weaving needles from the spruce
For visions we've embossed
On every hill and frozen lake
On windows, roofs, with mirth
"Ah look!" we cry, "Our masterpiece!"
A winter windblown earth.

KO THREAT
"When armies are mobilized and issues joined, the man who is sorry over the fact will win." Lao-tzu

One eye of mine fears the stones
(Deceitful simplicity of white and black)
Despising those that cannot live.
I hear the cadence of liberties at night
Clacking teeth of a tiger's mouth
A smell of sweat on glass
The immutable leer of White's *joseki,*
And I am black.
I peer at star points
Connect and cut and spin
Into the board, confused by nested mirrors,
Unsure which face is mine
Unclear about what's vital
Knowing the game plays me.

One eye of mine desires the stones
Cheers fingers that lust for touch and capture
Admires iron pillars that stand
And the posture of knights a thousand years past.
Melodious invasion, snapping back into key
Veering for artful *fuseki*
And patterns vaguely glimpsed
Through veils of *sente* worn
By seers who promise me hope
And handicaps.

We need two eyes to live:
An iris of terror, a lens of love,
Merely made of stones
And there is something here I do not understand.

SEPARATION

Running ridges on the thunderheads
With ozone-fractured sight
Purified by summer rain
From ragged rolling skies
Thinking of a winter friend
Who charmed the colder days
Through dim November window panes
I slipped into her heart
Melting icy streams that feed
A dry and thirsty tilting land.

Shearing round the mountain peaks
In sprays of blowing snow
Skirting talus in the gale
Where eagles rule misty stone
Wishes thriving soaring free
Straining for the source
Of all that pleads for life while
Shouting with the lightning bolts
And kneeling with the sleeping deer
In woodlands of the night.

I stand alone before the storm
She's not close by tonight
But still I'm sure of tenderness
Imagining her touch I know
We share the same sweet hymns
And love the same soft rain.

VESPERS

I no longer beg Jesus
For that or this
Or wonder why he should
Fret for sparrows
Or bliss out over non-vanilla wafers
But I still pray
And fervently
Though my missal is ashes
And our Bible anchors dust
Where I finally wearied of
Strong's Exhaustive Concordance
The bloody cross and criss
Of 'aleph and alpha, oh my god,
But I still pray
And kiss sacred icons
That are invisible
And do not hiss for silence
When joy demands noise
And sorrow craves no dogma
And it is not amiss to doubt
That all sparrows die famously,
I pray less than I piss
But prayer is no less needful.

I no longer delve into mysteries
As if I can *know*
Or was one of The Twelve, as written,
But I still pray
And focus
On the tears that water awe,
Could be bodily fluids and brain juice
Merely brewed and blended
In heart and veins and glands
But I still pray
Acknowledging, grateful, sad,
A subject in the domain

Of biology, though rebellious
And stubbornly sure
That human heads are haunted
And even Cain was loved.

BABYLON

Proselytes with venom spoor
A sophistry of hate
To sanctify the pyrrhic gods
Where brigands lie in wait.

Amulets of wenches
Oracular and tin
Smoking from the plastic forge
On goathead flights of whim.

Provender for crowded tombs
An acid for the veins
Rectal sounds of worship
Sebaceous oily gains.

Conjuring a holiness
To gluttons of the kill
Howlers of a lunar blood
To mummify the swill.

Narcosis of the fingertips
And hypodermic lies
To petrify the orphan hearts
And ossify their minds.

Palaver for the weary ears
Pentagonal with doubt
Revolvers for the weary heads
To blow the maggots out.

FINAL EXAM

Prophets grilled him
Under hot white lights
Of awareness
Demanding to know:
"When?"
A glaring indictment piercing like shards
Of broken glass
But owning an edge of fairness
They ask:
"How have you loved?"

YOUNG LOGGER

Branding axe in flashing sun
And steel cables taut
With vigor gleaming through the sweat
On tanned and weathered brows
Not cheaply bought
But aches and blood
Ignored in the roar of smoking diesels
And songs of hot and hungry saws
That whine of the danger of death
Well fought
On tumbling stacks of logs.

With weary thighs and ragged boots
He reveled in the madness
Often sought
And thrived in perilous jungles.

STORMY CITY BLUES

Streetlamp haloes diffused by rain
Hardened by asphalt shine
A flash of headlight glare
Silhouettes
Strands of power lines
That channel the vim of the slimy city
Rain-slicked and thunderstruck
Hollow mutterings roll
A slash of wind
Cuts drives wet-cold
Through matted hair on clammy scalp
Squishing shoes on cracked concrete
Running streams of turbid gutters
Spin and tumble soggy leaves
To grated sewers that have no end.

I trudge, I count the tarnished signs
As drizzle permeates my bones
Rhythmic drippings from the bricks
Of buildings senseless yet
Still whispering
"Alone."

A burst of yellow daffodils
An image in my brain
Wordsworth *lonely as a cloud*
But clouds aren't lonely in the rain
That without pity flails the city
For murkiness and sudden chills
Mocking warmth and sunshine whims
So foreign to the city storm
Which in the static grumbling thunder
Spouts and pours and pouts
"Alone."

No one on the curbs and walks
But wet and beaded meters
Stand starkly still in electric mist
Screaming *Violation!* in their eyes
Though a few with time left offer hope
That someone yet resists
Or at least that someone tries.

NIGHT SHIFT BARD

An astronaut of hyperspace
A basket case at night
Demanding from a turbid brain
Sweet lyrical delight
Will find that in the fervor
Of galvanizing dreams
Harsh heirlooms of his heritage
Still push in at the seams.

Insurgent though the will may be
To tame a jeering pen
Calliope will rise and wink
Then waft away again.

So latent and lamentable
No lover for the muse
Look: the stanza or the shovel?
You know which one to choose.

BLUE COLLAR

As loggers come
As loggers go
Hell,
We weren't so awful rough.
Tired, content
At end of shift
With two beers and day-old snuff.

THE SUNDOG CONSPIRACY

Beware you men who rule the world
With pathogenic ways
And pique its lust with pyrite baals
To nurse the souls of slaves.
All folk are not within the grasp
Of commerce, rites, and trends
There is no way to seal their graves
With fates that empires send.

As moonbeams in a silent pool
The Sundogs cruise the night
Forced into alleys, shadows, and woods
By money, greed, and might.
Resigned to nothing but abysmal hope
Not least but surely last
They serve the ones who read the stars
And illuminate the traps.

Beware you fools who rape the earth
For justice merely winks
Your crimes are not unseen, untold
But shouted in the streets.
And watch the dark when Sundogs roam
Parhelions of light
And dig your holes in rocks and hills
When midnight skies are bright.
For your castles and your kingdoms
Your lackeys and your priests
Will burn as hellish brimstone
Beneath the Sundogs' feet.

PROFESSIONAL WRITER

That folder wasn't the one
I needed
But it leaped into my hand
I swear, and none other
Wished for on a working morning
Was so damned thick with memory
So careless with minutes.
I should've spurned temptation
But I needed
More muse than I guessed
And stared at the penmanship
Of an adolescent
Drunk on Yeats, only rare as a Beatles fan
In Sixty-Five.

An hour lost, unpaid by publishers
And a neglected screen
Glaring with fresh green words
Bound to income and a Schedule C
But bearing no more love than
The scrawls in the folder
I needed
To write so badly when
My upstairs teen-aged room
Was an ivory tower.

CLASS OF '69

On the road to Canaan in nineteen-sixty-nine
Lured on by youthful appetites
And Dylan's heady wine
We caught the sounds of silence slamming in the marble
    halls
Where we would plumb the mysteries
If only we had the balls.
Sweet freedom in our little rooms away from home and
    mother
But we weren't really bad boys
Just bad for one another.
Storm the classes! Storm the books! Listen to the
    profs
Hear what high school told us
While we were jerking off.
Lead us, heal us, tell us what *They* thought
Show us life and purpose
No! you magi can't be lost.
For you don't see what Simon says, we ran to you for
    hope
If not here, ink on hands
We'd be Out There on a rope.
Get us high, feed us words, what is the flag you're
    flying?
We're not afraid of death at all
But we're scared to death of dying.
Darwin, Kant, and Hegel; Skinner, Plato, Fromm
Quickly! Tell us their minds
Before *They* use The Bomb.

On the road to nowhere in nineteen-seventy
For we couldn't flush the masters
From amid the heirs' debris.
The marble halls had failed us and who could understand
That Dylan's just a dreamer
Like every other man.

THE VOYAGEUR

The *Voyageur* hugging shore
Green wave awash the bow
Leaning on the forward rail
A slave to foggy mornings.

Around the point, flash of rocks
Now bucking northern wind
A gust of spray and frosty breath
To make the coffee sweeter.

Lichened cliff to starboard
Wisps of beacon light
Mournful gulls on outward wings
Dead ahead for Thunder Bay.

SHUFFLING THE TAROT DECK

It's not sorrow or fear
Nor a fatal blue funk
That narrows his evening to fantasies of deicide.
But impatience with tomorrow and today
And the keen sweet aroma of yesterday's ashes,
A tarot of old entries
Into journals, vaginas, and contracts.
Or maybe it's merely a good nap he needs
In some musty barrow or mound
Where sleep is a tonic to bones
Defended by the Knight of Wands and
Weary to the marrow with heroes
Whose courage is translucent
But heavy, demanding, damp and only borrowed
For the span of a sound bite
Broadcast by gunpowder.
Better, he believes, to be a sparrow
For only the instant it takes
To feel feathers and flight
And see if a nap might be
More refreshing than the Ace of Cups.

THE SWIMMING BEAR

Misty twilight hour
Dusky amber gray
So burdened by the forest
Shadowed from the sky
Beneath the dripping aspen
Rich green and rainy brush
Say vespers for the fading day
And let the black night come.

    The swimming bear is coming
    From cold and rocky shores
    Abreast the northern islands
    That smell of pine and furs.

Before the winter let us drink
And cruise the dormant woods
Salute the distant April sun
And lest we be so rude
Toast the nearing Arctic wind
For grace to live and last
"One more winter!" let us dream
Until the snow is past.

    The swimming bear is coming
    To rule foggy dawns
    And join the river echoes
    Where stars and clouds are drowned.

November's at the chimney top
For a draft molten birch
September died a month ago
On the prow of my canoe
The paddle's in the corner dry
Lakes are gone to ice
High the winter moon will sail
To grant the snow its crown.

The swimming bear is coming
On nights of frosty zest
To huff on evening embers
And wane into the west.

I heard a wolf last night
Out beyond the northern forty
It froze me quiet-still
Beneath the polar star.

The dreaming bear is coming
Along a great divide
Where ghosts of red men hover
And ravens waft and glide.

MIND SEARCHING

Into the mall of wreckage
Smoking sodden stench
Where twisted wings had gouged the earth
I came to study broken men.

One lay heaped where she had died
Discarded by the wind
Her skull split open to the sky
As if to gasp the last
And crouching low I peered within.

Shattered brain like marmalade
A lifeless ooze of slime
What happened to the pangs of love
What happened to the dreams
Surely I would find some words
Spilled out upon the ground
Ideas lying here and there
Forced out into the smoke.

I picked and prowled where she'd been tossed
And hunted scattered thoughts
No concepts smoldered in the trash
No doubts were strewn about.

I searched the wreckage through the night
But found no errant mind.

YELLOWSTONE AND STARS

I had a dream of General Grant
Of Traveler and Lee
Of Appomattox Courthouse spring
And what I yearn to see
Before this brindled century
So fresh and yet so vile
Spins out its final sortilege
And weaves a bitter smile
On lips that ever tasted brass
And transmutated hymns
From odes on God and Grecian urns
To advertising whims.

I had a dream of Crazy Horse
Of Sitting Bull and Gall
A Milky Way of buffalo
That rumbled like a squall
On plains as seas with tidal waves
Of grass and fire and breath
A nexus to the summer sky
And welcoming the death
That promised life through winter nights
With meat and hides and tales
No turpitude of severed tongues
None forked, no parchment veils.

I had a dream of Walden Pond
Of Yellowstone and stars
Of Clark and Lewis facing grizz
And fording sandy bars.

GOLDEN IRON SONG

Iron ranges, hands of steel
Born a miner's son
With pick axe forged into his fist
Dynamite between his teeth
Red ore dust on worn out rugs
Night shift whistles coaxing sleep
For children born to work.

Unrelenting railroad cars
Half-a-mile of hungry maws
Fed with iron and miners' sweat
Early pensions, bitter tears
Drilling rigs and huffing shovels
Race against (with autumn fears)
The Minnesota snow.

Miners' kids in shafts and pits
Sons of sons to dig
The red and yellow cliffs for life
To fill the Great Lakes ships.

A child peered beyond the dust
He heard beyond the roar
With books he soared to clustered stars
Draglines molted to dragons
Poems swelled like blossoms
He sipped from silver flagons
Forged in worlds of his own.

"You will not be a miner"
A mother's mantra-wish
She knew of scaling stockpile dumps
That never reached the sky
Where northern wind and sailing visions
Far too bright and high
Insisted on the clouds.

"You will not be a miner"
He sternly had been told
But felt condemned to hunt and scrape
For scattered flecks of gold.

FARAWAY WOMAN

Bewitching glimpse of a lonely beach
And a faraway woman with me
A restless yen, a stab of pain
As a breaker rolls in from the sea.

The faraway woman extends me her hand
I clasp, then let it slip free
She sighs with regret creased into her face
As a breaker rolls in from the sea.

She's striding away, tracks in the sand
I can't stop her though nothing stops me
I'm bashed to my knees, dragged out with the tide
As a breaker rolls in from the sea.

HER DOG!

Her dog! Her dog!
His tongue lolling out
She left him leashed
Someone cut it no doubt
What evil boy
Abetted his rout
And chased him down the alley?

She tied him and thought
He was safe in his pen
Who did this?
They'd better not do it again!

ROGUES AND TOADS

We cruised the Texas nights
Heavy-laden but happy
Mingling with the dew in forest mornings
While the moon had found
The rats and poultry dying.
We praised with beer-soaked laughter
Revealing ourselves and buddies
Via Bibles and red-mud backroads
Sweating our courage and bleeding the years
Heating like engines, filthy as toads
Kindled by one spark
Born of the fiery pistons of youth
Still without wings and hiking
Thumbs-out on rain-slicked highways
To coasts and kingdoms of sand.

In pews of the ditches
Before cement altars
We crawled and dug and sweat
Cursing the clay and a dollar-sixty an hour
While lunch emerged from the lagoon
Where most of our heroes lived.

We ran for our lives, our hearts
And more than our lungs
Ripped marathons out of the road,
Panchromatic pilgrims
With lenses for eyes and film for a fix
We inscribed our souls in silver
And heard the paeans of friends.

Pickups waxed glorious and quietly died
Good times faded to good old times
And brothers slipped from headlocks
Into legends of ancient semesters
Built of milk and honey and concrete block

Mortared with names and faces
Faces and names
Cured into the cells of our brains
Forever.

FIRST SEMESTER, LAST SEMESTER

Crumbling, crumbling
The new day withers on
Past many dried up river beds
Still dearth of wine and song
Where dusty currents rush the banks
That lately were so green
And only summer alchemy
Was there or could be seen.

Marching, marching
The hours clamor on
Projected by the shadow's shade
Still going to be gone
Where stones describe infinity
To sand of ancient years
And autumn's bright astrology
Foretells the winter fears.

Teeming, teeming
The anthills taper on
Grazing where the desert grows
Still conquering the lawn
Where grasses only dream to be
Where seeds are ill at ease
And April's fertile virgin
Has no phallic lust to please.

Slicing, slicing
The sunlight angles on
Cutting shorter deeper days
Still hinged within the dawn
Where only light will dare to pass
Across the roasting ground
And many shriveled brains will fry
With haughty sizzling sound.

DELUSIONS OF GRANDEUR

I desire a rapid death, that is
Buried in white water
Amidst the spartan waves and rocks
A bold and wild slaughter.

Northern river, reckless cold
Spewing spray and foam
Beneath a tumbling spruce-top sky
A hundred miles from home.

FIRST JUMP

Coils of fear constrict my chest
Harness, D-rings, risers
I really have a parachute
Weighing heavily, at best
Some say, a token of my youth.
Our helmets touch, the master speaks:
"The exit form my boy,
 Do it right you got it made
 Blow it and you're screwed!"
A chute could be a costly grail
For one who's not so oily old,
With adrenaline dreams of tearing wind
Grasping, snapping at jeans
Extended from the gaping door
Three thousand feet above the grass
Heart drumming, caring for more
Beyond the conscious scope
Of whitened fingers clutching
Or eagle's talons gripping
The angled strut.

"GO!"

I went.

I went! I'm gone! Unfurled silk
A blur of earth, I'm free!
I'm high! The horizon leaps
It's done, a billowing cloud my own
The Cessna eye-level in the sky
In the sky!
I'm an osprey—no, a man
To whom the clouds will never be the same
In the sky! Not under but *in*
I'll float I'll fly I will I can.

Let us laugh, let us pray:
"Hail Canopy, full of air
The wind is with thee
Blessed art thou of ripstop nylon
And blessed is the fruit of thy dangling toggles.
Holy Harness, absorber of shock
Always support us
Now and at the moment of out PLF
Amen."

Life!   I lust you!
Filled with air, yet dare
I live and love and give
To the full?
Swinging from puppet strings
Or maybe a nylon noose
Of indulgent design born of disdain
For trials and breath and stings
In the warp of a pitiless world.

The sky is so quiet at two thousand feet
I'm sure if I wanted to try
Ears echoing silence out to the blue haze
I'd be able to hear angels sigh.

"Airborne! Airborne! Have you heard?
We're gonna jump from the big-ass birds!"

Reality converges,
The earth with open fields
Reaches for my jump boots
And like other thrills I know this leap
Will often seem surreal
With pangs of fruitless strivings
After wind without a name
My lips won't even part to kiss
Or offer cheeks of tears to water thirsty hearts.

A recruiting poster says:
"When you jump, it's just you."
But that's bullshit, man
She was jumping too.

I struck the earth, embraced the dirt
Sprang up in jubilation
Learned to skip again and fell, blissful.
I see the sky where I have soared
From ground and grass but high, I'm high!
I tread the clay where I was born,
It never hinted I could fly.

To sing my joy into the clouds
Is easy fluently
But skies and lovers aren't the same
They listen differently.

RESTROOM WALLS

I am far away from me
You can't reach out to touch
With fairy tales of tender fingers

Is there very much

In rhythmic creakings of a bed
And rhymes of skipping rope
In children laughing in the sun
With wondrous dirty jeans?
Lovers loom as ruts that crush
Through fields of August clover
Only wicked as a logger's saw
That rips into his leg

I have to clutch

At proverbs on a restroom wall:
"There's no such thing as gravity the whole world
                    sucks."

You are far away from you
I can't reach out to touch
With myths and lies however white
There isn't very much
To read in books and faces
Or on the restroom walls.

THE HOLLOW TREE

When all along the velvet path
The moonlight spiders shine
You'll find us in The Hollow Tree
All stoned on autumn wine.

Who cares when cold the waves must be
Our tunes are warm and yellow
Who cares that ice will frame the door
And blizzards bawl and bellow.

For in the glow of firelight
We pass the pipe around
And clink our mugs in merry jest
Rejoicing at the sound.

To be a bard, to be a bard
Is not to be a nerd
And singing in The Hollow Tree
Is not to be unheard.

We lift our voices to the roof
Our spirits rise in time
And in our reason for the song
There is a joyful rhyme.

To each his own, the minstrel says
And some there are who know
That lilting rhyme and metered song
Will make the lotus grow.

SIGNS

On looking back you aged man
How do the signs appear?
Are they merely shapes without the words
That faded, never clear?
Or do you know them all by heart?

INTRODUCTORY ASTRONOMY

Planet Venus bright and keen
Glitters in an empty bowl
Upturned, viridian
And at one foci standing small
A child writes:
You cannot see the stars by looking up
Though alpine air of hardened glass
Is frozen cold and clear
Gazing up is not enough
Look *out* to see the stars
And think:
I am not the center.

WE RODE THE SOLAR WIND

Loamy soil pressed by hands
Caressing microbes
Squeezing worms
A fleck of leaf, roots of grass
Grains of crystal sand.

      Galactic nights between the stars
      We rode the solar wind
      To catch a breath of comets' tails
      Where no one else had been.

Cool rain from cotton clouds
Wetting lips
Feeding trees
Moistened stone, spattered lake
A life-sustaining kiss.

      The Moon had turned her secret face
      And Saturn spun away
      We saw that lights were blinking on
      All across the Milky Way.

Sunlight dapples nurtured fields
Spreading warmth
Injecting rays
A budding stalk, ripe flowing sap
A rich and staple yield.

      We listened to the pulsar song
      A million light years trip
      In nebulae of stellar gas
      New suns were born and lit.

BORN AGAIN

Smearing luscious blood
On gowns all lathered in moonlight
And on rocks washed in wind
Feverish with two thousand delirious dreams.

No, Shadow-Mother, no
Milk is only for never.

PAMELA

I

I knelt to sip from a mirror pond
On a dry and lonesome quest
And in the sheen observed a face
Not mine, but yours
And with a tender yearning
I dipped into your life.

II

Out of a chilling mist
You approached with a glow in your palms
My heart was damp and hollow
Weary of battling the gods.
You pressed your lips to stone
And coaxed it into flame
Then slipped into my arms
And laid with me until morning.

III

A poem was scribed on the windy beach
To salve the sand? To still the waves?
I read a gull and heard it reach
And grasped its joy as my own.
You drew the poem, I sensed your faith
With fingers not feathers you spoke
And listening to the surf I find
A seagull recited the words.

IV

Two ravens soared before the storm:
I thought of you and I.

AUGUST 16TH, A SUNDAY

A nuance of the wildwood
Elusive as a wolf
Will only fracture like the rock
And only cling as lichens
To the surface of my sight
Where starry nights have shone through mist
And mournful loons have cried
Or did they laugh?

A nuance of the wildwood
As tortured as the trail
Will only wave like gusts of wind
And only waft as pollen
Through the meadows of my sight
Where stormy nights have raged till dawn
And darkness battled light
Or did they kiss?

A nuance of the wildwood
As fleeting as the foam
Will only rift like bubbles
And only wash as waves
Across the beaches wide and low
Where chilling surf has churned the sand
And winter goblins go
Or do they come?

Yes, they come.

AFTER BIBLE STUDY

Hail to the eve of sordid war!
Spurring the black horses
Onto plains of blood
Amid horns of battle
Sabers glinting under the moon
Our burnished helms a flood
Where Guards of the Holies
Fell in smoking heaps by guns
Sooty, mired in gory mud.

Roar with triumph!
Songs of combat on our pale lips
Firing and slashing in deadly haze
Forward! To the crest! No quarter!
As swords of vengeance bite and blaze.

BELSHAZZAR

Accelerating into haze
On a bat with smoking wings
Contemplating all the while
Concentric benzene rings
That scorch the writing on the wall
But do not burn the hand,
Another brew in the midnight
Cry: "Daniel! Daniel! He's our man!"

MICHELE'S OTHER FACE

Like a ship drummed by storm
All inside she is warm
Though the breakers are trying to drown her.
With a Siamese cat
And a book on her lap
She smiles at the photos of brothers.
Though her ego is frail
There is more to the tale
She'll be plucked by a man while she listens.
Her lips cry "no pain!"
But I can smell rain
She's grasping for something that's missing.
Her mind's insecure
And the smile is unsure
She's groping for rocks in the current.

We watched from the heights
Imagining flights
To the moon rising amber below us.
We slid down from our high
And she kissed for a sigh
She is spinning in eddies of laughter.
We offer our care
For as far as we dare
It is simple to reach her and love her.
She kindles our eyes
With her cheerful disguise
She's a sister to hard lonely brothers.

ADVISOR TO THE KING

I saw a spider down in Hell
Or was it in my hand?
I peered behind the curtain
And my eyes were stung by sand.
A seagull swirled past the moon
And blessed the purple sun
I staggered on the barren beach
And dropped my shattered gun.

I listened to the royal horn
(I wish I had the tape)
In poems to the new-crowned king
I accused his court of rape.
While bearing gifts unknown to them
The royal members came
Their voices rasped of mutant men
But their robes were still the same.

I crouched upon a sunlit beach
The spider in my hand
The king had drawn the curtain
But my eyes were cleansed of sand.

WINTER LOVE

The snow has lightly brushed my hand
Deceived my trusting core
I thought the snow was warm, not cold
I thought she loved me more.

The snow is sighing tenderly
And white with purest ends
To gild the earth with crystal
And the sleep that winter sends.

Snow beckoned to her drifted woods
That sparkled in the sun
The trees had bowed beneath her grace
The streams had ceased to run.

And there she left me freezing
Where ice had cracked below
The snow will only love you
When you love the snow.

WEDDING RAIN

Rain beat on the windows
An organ boomed within
Where he cast his determined monumental "I do"
      into her shimmering eyes
Despite the rumbling din.

The pastor turned a shepherd's face
With anointed arc he welded:
"Till galaxies are cosmic dust blown by a
      breathless wind of the universe
Till frozen moons are melted."

The shepherd raised his weary eyes
To lambs as yet unborn
What meaning for a wedding day!
Amid the clouds and storm.

For the organ boomed within
And rain beat on the windows.

COSMOLOGY

Sometimes on cold winter nights
As I watch smoke surge billow and twist
From dozens of blunt chimneys
and diffuse before the frigid stars
I wonder about death.

That is
I wonder if it would be better to freeze
To death or be poisoned.
Of course it's silly thought
I'd rather die under a clear sky than be killed.

I understand chimneys
But why are there stars?

PROGRESS

Gross domestic cogs and wheels
Cannot evade the law
And fashion towers to the stars
Or delay the coming beacon
Or hide what Noah saw.

That granite is so delicate
So soluble in stress
When catastrophic destiny
Called in to kill and cleanse
Can surely do no less.

Trees cry out for mercy
Rivers burn and plead
Birds rot on their perches
Having never learned a dirge
Having never seen the need.

Belly-up parboiled frogs
Enhance a putrid ditch
Resin-coated meals of death
For oil-painted ducks
For nightmares of a witch.

A journey to the stars for us?
Alas, the sky's opaque
The moon a hazy orb of gray
A smudge upon the night
A phantom in the lake.

THE FOE

Come meet the foe
You learn to kill
And you become a killer.
Come meet the foe
You twist the law
And you become a shyster.
Come meet the foe
You learn to lie
You become a politician
Come meet the foe
And when you win
You become the foe.

THE JOKE

I

A sacrifice was called at night
A boy died in the dark
How funny was the tragic scene
How tragic was the joke.

A laugh was snared along the ground
The humor wasn't lost
How aching was the final line
How final was the joke.

A wake was held amidst the trees
The boy was seen by crows
How wayward was the raucous noise
How raucous was the joke.

II

We all could see the boy was dead
A limerick to the last
And Death that slapstick master
Took a bow as we all laughed.

Oh, Death, you personality
Your style claims renown
You can be seen most any day
You thrive. You are a clown.

We howled with glee as Death glanced up
He objects to being ribbed,
For the boy you see was merely dead
But Death had never lived.

FULL MOON: JUST A PHASE

Serf's up!
In this harvest of humus
Where serenity is only a guest
And seniors yearn for baptism
Into unspent youth
But sewn loafers and idol practices
Keep watched ovens from baking
A convenient peace negotiated
By shoestring patricians
Plus Sister Veranda
She of the cornbread vespers
And beaming potatoes
Over which we intone "Rye? Wry?"
In the neighborhood of nothing
There's always a chance of flurries
Spit by the Queen of Clouds
And grinning with an iron mouth
About the foolish mantra of Mr. Big
Somehow overheard in the osprey's nest
Or under a pedestal
Sounding a little revolting
In the secret files of the sisterhood
Via simulcast nightmares
Of the metropolitan suburban safari
That comedy of good deeds etched
On a chart of the moon's far side
Where we never know what time to tell
Or say to Mickey and Pluto
With Liquid Paper and molten words
In a great American love letter
Abandoned on an anthill and dubbed
"The Old Tavern Trilogy"
Or was it something by Vonnegut?